Dear Dave

I'm so happy to
share this I hope
it gifts you where
you need. Life, Joy & Love

Romeo
2018

OTHERED

Sibling Rivalry Press, LLC
PO Box 26147
Little Rock, AR 72221
info@siblingrivalrypress.com
www.siblingrivalrypress.com

ISBN: 978-1-943977-55-0

Library of Congress Control No. 2018941799

This title is housed permanently in the Rare Books and Special Collections Vault of the Library of Congress.

First Sibling Rivalry Press Edition, September 2018

ARKANSAS
QUEER POET
SERIES
#1

OTHERED

Randi M. Romo

SIBLING RIVALRY PRESS
LITTLE ROCK, ARKANSAS
DISTURB / ENRAPTURE

INTRODUCTION

The first time I read poetry in public, at a open mic as part of the Arkansas Literary Festival, Randi M. Romo was there. She was there the second and third times, too, pulling me into LGBTQ community events in Central Arkansas, where inevitably she'd be surrounded by queer youth with and without homes, with and without parents, and with and without self-worth, each of these kids looking at her knowing she would look back at them and really see them.

She'd never say it herself, and she'd downplay it if it were said in her presence, but Randi saved the lives of a lot of LGBTQ youth in my home state. She saved the lives of a lot of LGBTQ adults, too, creating formal and informal social-support and mental-health networks to benefit an overlooked and often-neglected segment of the Arkansas population.

Like so many Arkansans, Randi is a storyteller. More than that, Randi is a *witness*, which I believe is the magical part of the equation in storytellers that turns them into poets. She's pulled to serve as witness and provide voice for people who have been made to feel less than, or silenced, or othered. Sometimes those voices belong to kids she's had a hand in saving. Sometimes those voices belong to kids who couldn't be saved, even with her best efforts. Sometimes those voices come from her own mirror, where laugh lines and scars are proof of battles won and lost and of loved ones here and gone.

When I think of queer poetry in Arkansas, I think of the queer poets who create it and nurture it out of a sheer need to survive. I think of how, when an othered poet stands in a room full of friends and strangers and finds the courage to share their work, there's always someone in the audience needing a dose of courage, too. I think of how there's always someone in the crowd needing to be seen. That's the power of poetry: to witness.

Randi's poetry reminds me of our radical, queer sisters who wrote in the 70s and 80s; those poets who fought the fight so new generations, including my own, could be seen today. Randi's seen so many of us that I wanted to turn the tables and create a space where we see her. I can think of no person better representative of the spirit I want the Arkansas Queer Poet Series to carry than my friend and fellow witness, Randi M. Romo. This book represents a small portion of what she's seen.

– Bryan Borland
Publisher, Sibling Rivalry Press

DEDICATION

This book is dedicated to ALL who have been "othered" by policies, laws, institutions, pulpits, and bullies. It is in memory of those who did not survive the struggle; those who died silent deaths in the throes of the consequences of being seen and treated as other. Those taken by violence and those by their own despair— because they were othered. This book is for all those who have survived and those who remain in struggle. It is a hope that we can learn to truly see one another and find our most common element: humanity.

This book is also to remind those who are seen and treated as other to consider the ways they, too, see and treat some as other. The badge of one's particular oppression is not a free pass to contribute to the oppression of anyone.

Othered is also dedicated to my beloved daughter, whose life was deeply impacted by the penalties of otherness and who paid the ultimate price, with her life.

– Randi M. Romo

Jennifer Lea Bearden
June 9, 1974 – February 4, 2018

TABLE OF CONTENTS

NO WHITE AFTER LABOR DAY

Your suits were as proper
as any worn by Jackie Kennedy
pill box hat
gloves that matched
high heels
your value
measured in children born
shiny house
the husband
a worth you thought your only legacy

for me

the oldest
and only daughter
who must inherit

Little did you know
the steel you forged in the midst
of the bony trail of my spine
it held me true to the me that
terrified you
as I learned from the best
as I bore all the pain

that filled your heart
spewing angry raging words and fists
as you railed at all of me that was imperfect
inside the tiny little frame
they fooled you into believing
was all there was for you

WARRIOR WOMAN

Lori Piestewa
White Bear Girl
only 23 in desert fatigues
she rode toward her economic opportunity
a poor woman gone to fight
with other poor people
in a war she didn't start
for a regular paycheck
healthcare and a chance at a better life
for herself
her boy and her baby girl
both who would never again
feel the touch of their mother's hand
upon their face or know her songs
as they fell asleep beneath the peak
named Squaw by men with white skin
in the place where the lands of the first people
the Hopi and the Navajo meet
land that is rock and dust and grows
little hope and the word future
really means unemployment and poverty
that grinds away at the lives
of those decimated
by the loss of their lands
forced religion and government schools

this woman colored in the line of her need
with army green and desert tans
shouldering a rifle to follow the path
of her father and grandfather who had served
the stars and stripes
going to Vietnam and World War II
filled with patriotism and their own hopes
of economic opportunity mixed with
the ghosts of their ancestors who had resisted
that same flag's arrival upon their sacred lands
following a path that was slippery
with the loss of dreams and conquered hopes
and as her life's blood painted the Iraqi sand
the poor were still poor
the rez was still there
and her kids would get her army check for
dying her hero's death
scared and alone in a foreign country
looking for weapons of mass destruction
that never existed
and it's pretty damn sad that it took her death to
remove the name Squaw
from the peak that overlooked her hometown
and no matter the posthumous medals
the ceremonies
or the naming of a mountain

none of this will bring her back to her family
who will always be without their loved one
who died because the best job
that White Bear Girl could find
was carrying a gun
and marching
for Uncle Sam

A GAME OF WASHERS

It's a little past sunset at the farm
Thanksgiving eve
and the stars are creeping out
poking holes
in the nighttime sky
with little neon bright pinpricks of light

Pickup trucks of all kinds
sit parked in a half-circle
their tailgates down with
a cooler on the end of each
the fire pit is stacked
high with wood and it's
all ablaze with flames
crackling and popping
spitting heat like
mad beats

There's a speaker on the porch
blasting out old-school country music
and in between those songs there's
Mexican Cumbias
Rancheros
and Banda

Cousins of all hues
stand around in camouflage coveralls
their breath steaming clouds in the cold
Oklahoma night air
waiting their turn to pitch
in a game of washers and
all the while there's a
steady stream of trash talking
punctuated with the crack
of another cold one opened
while each in their turn
squints in the dim light
taking careful aim and lets metal fly
making a constant thumping bass line
as the heavy discs
hit the game board's wooden face

Over across the yard
the smoker is letting off clouds that smell
so good you can almost
taste the brisket in the air

My Tía pulls her chair closer to the fire
but no matter how hot it burns
it seems she always feels
the cold night air

My Tío smiles and puts on
another log while kidding her about
her icy feet in bed
the laughter paving the way for the
sudden breeze that pops up and pushes
across the top of the hill
scattering leaves and magic
before it and in this place
in this moment
with kith and kin
con mi familia
it is perfect

BABY BOY

Baby Boy
lost in that hurt that was ground into his skin
by a basher who yelled

Hey Faggot

before he beat the innocence out of his soul
the stars from his eyes and the
hope from his breath
sacrificial lamb to an altar
of bigotry
left lying in the dark
unconscious
and alone
painting
the ground
a blood-tinted
tribute of hatred
as his
dreams scatter
like crows
before the bang
of a shotgun

Baby Boy
watching
the guilty go free
while his own wounds of
flesh and heart
bored deep into the well
of his memory while he was
told one more time
that he doesn't matter
that justice isn't for all
that it's not
for the rainbowed
the same-gender loving
the gay, the queer
the dyke, the lesbian
and most especially
not for him

The Faggot

Baby Boy
so hurt, lost, afraid
and lonely
dancing on the
top of the edges
of razor blades

drinking straight shots of broken glass
trying to hang
onto barbed wire lifelines
trying so hard to live
trying so hard to die

trying to hang on

trying to hang on

until in quiet
desperation
he swings out
wide and free
flinging himself
into the void of
space
where he just
lets go with arms
widespread
sailing
through the sunset of his pain
coming in for a crash landing
into that promised land of
anywhere but where he was
even if it meant

not of this world
a land where
all that he is and
all that he ever
wanted to be
is just exactly

right

A place where the hurt could fall away clean
like ribs off the bone
all special sauced and tender
sweet, juicy
taste of freedom

But that which is God
Saint, Goddess or
Spirit said
Not yet, Baby Boy. Not yet
blowing the dust of death's requiem
from his nose
inflating his broken heart
to beat once more
to the drum of
possibility
that which is

more than he can see right now
perched up high
on his windowsill
of self-destruction

Old queer angels holding onto him
until the day that
he believes
in his
own right to be
human
queer
and loved

Nicholas "Nic" West
June 2, 1991 – April 5, 2018

WAS IT REALLY YOU?

Dreams

Did you have them
surely you did

Wishes

Did you conjure
spells to fulfill them

Hope

Did you keep refilling
the leaky cup
that bled your heart
as your life was
molded and shaped
by hands not your own

Did you dream your
mother alive again

Did you wish to be
exactly who you
wanted to be

Did you hope against hope
to be the Captain of your fate
Did you dream of us
all the children that came

Did you ever think
it would all go this way

Did you ever truly
get to do anything
that was just for you

THE NIGHT YOU DISAPPEARED

The screen door slammed shut
a rifle crack of sound that split the air
creating a silence so profound
it was as if the earth
and all she carried upon her face
had together of one accord
stopped breathing

And then the crickets
begin again and a
man on the front and one
on the rear carries you across the porch
their breath coming hard
as they lift you up and over the step
and you're so beautiful
eyes closed peacefully
hair a shining black halo
framing your silent face
stark against the white of stretcher sheets

I sit up high in my crow's nest of a
strange man's arms
peering over his shoulder
heady with the scent of his aftershave

Old Spice, I think
not really knowing what the tableau before me meant
as you disappeared into the gaping maw
of a white and red bubble-topped vehicle that
flashed and screamed you away from me / from us
into the void of night

I didn't know then the hurt that you carried so deep
that it was ground into the DNA of your
bones, your blood and your brain
silvery daggers of pain that cut
away your smile a little more bit by bit
until your teeth no longer saw the light of day

I didn't understand an agony that could
make you want to disappear

For a long time about that night I didn't remember
the ceremony of your preparations to leave us
how you bathed us and dressed us
all up in our Sunday best
my two brothers and I
how you sat us upon the sofa all in a row
so shiny and perfect
while you took yourself in your finest raiment
behind the bathroom door where with the click

of a lock you embarked upon your journey
no luggage needed as you swallowed
your one-way ticket

You came back one day
but not really
the absence
it was there in your eyes for a very long time

I missed you so much

Little did I know then
that missing you would
become a way of life

BLESS YOUR HEART

As a child there
was Spanish spoken
my mother's first
language and
then the English
of the fathers

There came a time
we moved away
from the land where
speaking Spanish
brooked no alarms
going to a place far
below the Mason-Dixon
in the deep South
to the people
of the second father
to find that another
kind of English was the native tongue

y'all was a noun
and a pronoun
and it could be
singular or plural

while bless your heart
was not meant to
seek the Lord's
intervention in the
care of your heart
rather as a means to
call one dumb as a bag of hammers
or unable to accomplish simple tasks
like finding your ass with both hands
in your back pockets

When telling grandpa
who was pretty old
that his fly was open he told me simply
that a dead bird doesn't fall from the nest

No matter what was about to be done
everybody was fixin' to

When telling Granny
any kind of untruth
she'd lean way back
and look you dead in
your eye and tell you
that dog won't hunt

The first time
one of the aunts said butter my biscuit
I went to the kitchen
to look for a biscuit and some butter

Uncles would tell you
that they might could
carry you to the store
but you'd have to wait
cause it was so hot that the chickens were
laying hard-boiled eggs

For a good long while
I didn't understand
what was being said

I'd smile and nod
trying to puzzle it out
in the context of all that had come before
but in the end it turned out alright

I got to where
I understood them pretty well

Excuse me now
I gotta get back to work

you know idle hands
are the devil's playground

But before you go
could y'all cut
them lights off
and make sure the
hose pipe ain't dripping

Y'all come back now

COMING OUT

Straining
gasping
pushes of birth,
coming out of the womb
shoulder
shrugging
arm reaching for freedom
coming out of the
last safe space
years till another
coming out
cruising the nurses
and if I'd talked
I'd have asked
for their numbers

Coming out all
idealistic
young and tender
embracing myself while
horrified parents
turned their faces and
crushed my heart
for coming out

They sent me away
locked me up
in the
crazy house
and inside schools for
queer exorcisms

For coming out
they denied me
they tore me
out by the roots
and still I came out
filled with tear-washed
stone slabs of resolve

And still
I stayed out
paying a price

That was not my debt
and here I am
at last
FREE
free to be
free to be me
free to be counted

free to fight
for the right
of coming out

DINNERTIME

Brown girl/White girl
all rolled into one
Mexican mama
and a white daddy
living in the South
¿Cómo se llama y'all?
all sewn together
at the dinner table
hot flour tortillas
beans and rice
tacos and tamales
pozole and chicken mole
enchiladas
fried chicken mashed potatoes
purple hull peas boiled cabbage
cornbread red velvet cake
eating our differences
at Sunday dinners
sopping up the casual racism
of aunties
with granny's fluffy biscuits
while at home it was mama's pain
wrapped in tortillas
buttery tears slipping out
and running down our arms

PLANTING SEASON

Grapefruits
I hate them
that was the size of the tumors
that took my boy and my man
funny thing they weren't blood
but in death they were the same

Strawberries
I hate them too
those were the fields where they worked
while a deadly gas
laid in wait for them trapped under tarps
getting the ground ready for the berries
They. Pulled. Up. The. Tarps.

After the funerals I start to hear
that this gas is so bad it's been banned
except for the strawberries and
except for some third world countries
with other brown skinned people
growing and picking
fruits and vegetables
to fill American grocery store bins
while grapefruit crops slowly blossom
inside the tiny farms of their loved one's brains

GOD, KUDZU, AND WHISKEY

She asked me why I tattooed angels
inside my eyelids
I told her so that I could always see
heaven
because I think God
has surrendered
taken up
drinking whiskey
smoking Kools
pack torn open
lucky smoke flipped upside down
a sigh exhaling
smoking rings
of complete dismay
at the human project
that has gone so awry
in the biosphere lab
called Planet Earth

Neither flood, fire, nor quake
no amount of love
ever enough to eradicate
the kudzu of evil that wraps hearts
and warps minds

harming the least and all the in-between
under the one percent
ground up for filling the belly of the beast
our bones, hopes and dreams

Our pre-existing condition
of being human
drawing breath
that is metered out by ability to pay
while the means hang far from reach
carrot on a stick
ice rattles in the glass
another match scratches out a light
two fingers more of golden contemplation

Behind my eyelids
angels sing on high
no place else
to sing their song

JESUS IS COMING

Homeless man
bearded and dirty
wandering the streets
eyes rolling in that
wild horse kinda way
singing chanting praying
all God's visions
that he sees brought
to him by a fiery chariot
so profound his belief
that anger wells within
that the masses cannot
see nor hear the gift
he shares from on high
louder he shouts of salvation
urgently he warns of demons
arms waving wildly
skinny black crow wings
making punctuation marks
at the people passing by
most shake their heads
hoping that he gets help
back on his medication
somehow someway someday

crazy old man always talking
'bout Jesus coming back
they need to lock him up
while every Sunday morning
in the pulpits of churches
stand the ordained the blessed
men and women of God
who bring the same message
of demons salvation and
the joyous return of Jesus
some preach sweetly
while others pound away
at the sinners in their midst
the church sings and sways
and all the people say amen
dropping dollars in the plate
full of their self-proclaimed
piety and respectability
some build churches like
impregnable fortresses
self-contained communes of
Jesus Loves You
bookstore gym coffee shop
restrooms with fancy soap
and heavenly soft two-ply
keeping the world at bay

until heaven's gate is nigh
locked up tight every night
to keep out homeless preachers
left to lie upon their concrete beds

FAN LETTER TO HEDY LAMARR

Dear Ms. Lamarr,

I know you don't know me
I'm just a kid over here
in a small Florida town with
honeysuckle sippy cups
hopscotch drawn on the sidewalk
trees leaning heavy with
oranges big as your head

It's hotter than blue blazes
most every month
and we got preachers by the
dozens shouting from pulpits
about sin and wickedness
and there are boys and girls
and we're all supposed to be
getting ready to pair up
and walk down the aisle
for the marrying ways

Still it doesn't feel quite right to me
this pairing of me and a him
I really didn't know why

I felt so different, so strange
till the day I saw your movie
Sampson and Delilah
I wasn't paying attention
to the television
but then your voice gave me

pause

I looked up to see you
draped with yards of fabric
that showed miles of skin
that glued me to the screen
as you struggled with your
beliefs and loving a lion-
wrestling strong man who heard voices

You. Were. Beautiful.

Each time you
spoke, moved
or stretched out in elegant repose
my heart beat faster
my stomach trembled
and warmth flowed through
inner sanctums that had

yet to occur to me
each new costume cleverly
conceived to excite my
thirsting eyes
so close I could touch you

and I wanted to

and it terrified me

and it exhilarated me

and I knew something
was forever changed on
a Saturday afternoon

Sincerely yours,

Your Biggest Fan

I AM

I am a woman
I am strong
I am a dyke

YOU'RE A SICK PERVERT

I am a child
a sister
an aunt
a lesbian

WHAT YOU NEED IS A REAL MAN

I am a mother
a nana
and butch

WHAT ARE YOU, A FREAK?

I am a friend
a worker
a homosexual

HOW COULD THIS HAPPEN IN OUR FAMILY?

I am a writer

an insomniac

a queer

YOU'RE GOING TO BURN IN HELL

I am a dreamer

a fighter

a sapphite

YOU'RE FIRED

I am an artist

passionate

a marimacha

BLOOD RELATIVES OR SPOUSE ONLY

I am spiritual

loyal

a lover of women

YOU'RE AN ABOMINATION TO GOD

I am confident

happy

gay

YOU
FILTHY
DEVIANT
WHORE

I AM (REPRISE)

The beginning lines of an old schoolyard chant
float through my brain
it wasn't true then and it's a lie now
that bullshit about sticks and stones

Words hurt
wounding tender hearts
that are torn by the verbal bullets
that spew from the lips of family and strangers alike

I hide the blood of my injured heart
masquerading as wet, shining tears
I will never show to those who
whip me bloody with the clubs
of ignorance and hatred
that hit me with hurricane force
threatening to embrace my hurt
in drink, drugs or flying high to the
freedom of God's angels' arms
from the highest rooftop
that I can find

I remember who I am
all that I am

and I straighten my back
anchor my soul
throw back my head
and howl
rejoicing
for I know that
I am more
than they will
ever see
beyond their
narrow little minds
their hatred
robbing their
very soul's grace
Rejoicing
yes
I am rejoicing
as I remember
all that
I am
rejoicing that
I am still here
rejoicing
because

I AM

I REMEMBER

the first time that my door creaked open in the night
the way he slid into my covers shushing my alarm
the fear that tripled the jackhammer beat of my heart
wild rabbit scared squirming to escape his arms

The quietly roaring screaming whispers of his threats
I will kill your brothers kill them all dead if you tell
I will kill you rip out your heart
and feed it to your mother
before I eat her heart and kill her as dead as you

The daytime it was as though nothing had happened
as if the blood on my sheets stigmata appeared
extra comics special treats new clothes trips to the store
payments for what was done to me in the dark of night

The shame / the fear / the loneliness / the hurt / the rage
swallowing my guilt like milk and cookies before bed
chair at the door tightly wrapped
little mummy in my quilt
unanswered prayers taught me that God wouldn't save me

Learning to sleep in boots jeans sharp-edged knife
reaching under my pillow for the second knife hidden

the last time that he came for me my armor he found
though he tried to reach through my blade

That no words were exchanged the blade at his throat
the agreement silently made that I would not kill him
slowly upright he sat on the side of my bed and wept
for what I couldn't tell the loss of his toy or death's proximity

The firestorm of madness ignited by those evening visits
as the fuel of grief-stricken insanity burned me to the ground
swimming to the bottom of 90-proof bottles only to drown
punching veins nostrils and lungs just please take me higher

The next man who touched me after him asked did I mind
blade in hand fury beyond words I assured him I did
the times after that men's hands caught me unawares
a dyke raped again to keep me in my woman's place

All of the raping touching grabbing pinching and leering
the nasty suggestions that they'd love to make real
tried a lot of places at a friend's or on the street or at work
a constant fight to keep prying evil hands and dicks away

Not a one of these things happened in a public bathroom
Not a one of these things happened in a public bathroom
Not a one of these things happened in a public bathroom

Not a one of these things happened in a public bathroom
Not a one of these things happened in a public bathroom
Not a one of these things happened in a public bathroom
Not a one of these things happened in a public bathroom
Not a one of these things happened in a public bathroom
Not a one of these things happened in a public bathroom
Not a one of these things happened in a public bathroom
Not a one of these things happened in a public bathroom
Not a one of these things happened in a public bathroom
Not a one of these things happened in a public bathroom
Not a one of these things happened in a public bathroom
Not a one of these things happened in a public bathroom
Not a one of these things happened in a public bathroom
Not a one of these things happened in a public bathroom
Not a one of these things happened in a public bathroom
Not a one of these things happened in a public bathroom
Not a one of these things happened in a public bathroom
Not a one of these things happened in a public bathroom
Not a one of these things happened in a public bathroom
Not a one of these things happened in a public bathroom
Not a one of these things happened in a public bathroom
Not a one of these things happened in a public bathroom
Not a one of these things happened in a public bathroom
Not a one of these things happened in a public bathroom
Not a one of these things happened in a public bathroom
Not a one of these things happened in a public bathroom
Not a one of these things happened in a public bathroom

JUST ME

The joy of me
the dyke
the pain of
me the daughter
sunlight through prisms
lighting my queerness
though
all the while
thunderclouds
of your disappointment
hung on the horizon
lightning strikes
of guilt
flung like Thor's hammer at my heart
that is never tough enough
to not feel the constant loss
of the dances
of reconciliation
that always totter off the
broken high heels
that held such great expectations
of what you thought it meant
to be female

the curlers
the makeup
dresses and skirts
wishing for me
dates with boys
the big wedding
a fine husband
and children galore
all the while
keeping yourself
blind to this living
standing right
in front of you
breathing child
both hands lifted in devout supplication
rendering invisible
the me that was
the me that is
and the me
that will never be
other
than the me
that I am
while you held
fast to your
fairytale dream

LOVE YOU FOREVER

Love You Forever
was a book I used
to read
to my baby's baby
this child that
I was raising
because I'd broken
my own into pieces
though I loved her
and never meant to

it was just
another verse
another ugly chapter
in the eternal story

hurt people

hurt people

broke her so bad

it's been years
since last we

tried to talk
to each other
in brittle conversations
that ran off the rails
in all the pain and despair
that I had fed her with
every bite of Gerber's
every bottle of milk
and every single second
that I was absent
self-medicating my way
through all of the bars
booze, drugs and
comforting arms that
I could find to bandage
my own bloody wounds
until all that was left of us
were these broken hearts

I often hate that
there came a time
I finally got better
because she didn't
and the guilt gnaws
holes the size of Texas
through my soul

each day
it makes me weep
for her, for us
for the we
that never was
for the hopes of
the we of someday
clinging to my life raft
the thought that
for as long as
we both shall breathe
there is hope
I love her forever
I always will

GOODBYE MY LOVE

Gray skies, the banner above
the black ribbon of asphalt
upon which you ride
enshrined in white and gold
an unnatural spring blooming atop

Following behind on your journey
desperate, these last moments
wretched beyond repair
green tent, standing sentinel below
as into the valley we go

Into my arms, the very last time
we carry you up that hill
struggling to bear the weight of this
as your children's tears anoint
standing at the edge of the abyss

I run through the litany of my sins
all of the ways that I failed you
like a razor-blade gauntlet
again and again and again
this terrible price of my imperfection

Tucking you into this Carolina hillside
as the cold, red clay falls atop
my heart slides in beside you
if only loving had been enough
I love you forever, I always will

Jennifer Lea Bearden
June 9, 1974 – February 4, 2018

SLAM

I wanted to be
up on this stage
all bad-ass slam poet
blowing you out
of your chairs
with my performing words
pulling you into my world
connecting us in a way that
the anchors of black ink
on bright white parasails
can simply never do
but alas I am forced to
limit the amazing
performance
the one I hear
and see inside my head
the one that would
thrill you all
make you lean in
afraid you will miss
one second
of what I have to say
I know I could have
been just that good
but I can't because I can't

memorize what I write
EVER!
Brain injury you see
but not because I rode
a bike without a helmet or
dove into a shallow pool
none of these things
gave me this leaky brain
that can never hold
what I write
without the prompts of pages
printed words
nailing me down
eye trying to send to brain
and out through my lips
some kind of honey flow
See it's like this
I got this brain by being sent
to a place, an institution
where they sent the mentally
incompetent, the mentally ill
the throwaways,
the kid that was me
and I was all of 13
not crazy, insane, nor mental
none of that, just... different
not different like
"my she seemed so normal"

No… it wasn't that kind
of different at all
it was… gay different
like "she likes girls" different
and it was while trying
to hold on to the vestiges
of my sanity trying to
survive the scariest
place on the planet
that my brain was
forever changed
It was while trying to
remember what it
felt like to be a kid
I chased a Frisbee
that had sailed away
high up onto a rooftop
my fellow patient
seriously miscalculating
the trajectory of her throw
although to be fair
it was easy to see
how she could miss
with eyes glazed and
muscles all spastic
from being
medicated to the nines
ALL of the motherfucking time!

So there I stood
for just a moment
atop this caged wall
face turned up to the sky
savoring the sweetness of
air and sun on my skin
that was not bound
behind the prison of fear
that was not confined
under lock and key
relishing
a peace that was
not hypodermically
induced
It was their shouts of
"RUNNER!"
that startled me
and turned me round
to see who, where
as my balance
gave way
I realized it was me
that they meant
just seconds
before my face
crashed into concrete
and I was longtime gone
until one day the blink

of my eye had meaning
because I understood
that it had blinked
and that I had returned
to this misery, this hell that
would be my home for
two more years where
I mastered resting bitch face
running pretty fast and the
art of physical combat
as a means of survival
inside this place
where my brain
was stamped and torn
but never
completely erased
So. With all that said.
I'm so sorry to say
you'll have to
endure me reading
my little poems
and stories to you

BLACKBIRDS IN FULL METAL JACKETS

When you wish upon a star
makes no difference who you are
Or. So they say...

In the land of the Magic Kingdom
where a tribe's pulse beat to the bass
the children danced
much the same
as I danced once upon a time
inside the bones of its ancestor

Those days so long ago
when we drank our courage
so as to drown our fear of all
that lay beyond those castle walls
disco ball a-twirling, spells cast
we danced to the Hustle
Love to Love You Baby
line dancing to Rapper's Delight
Ho-tel, Mo-tel, Hol-i-day Inn

Amazon warriors
atop platform shoes

armored in silk shirts
white pants creased
paper cut sharp
hair feathered into helmets
by Vidal Sassoon
and every single one
of us trying to hit
that Travolta strut
dancing to the BeeGee's
Stayin' Alive
as we all struggled
to do just that...
to stay alive

Closets were deep
filled with more
than winter coats
lives forced
upon cruel wire hangers
often wounded / often bloodied
hearts in constant arrhythmia
at being found out
at being thrown out
at being / at being / at being
but it was on that glittering dance floor
that we exhaled, that we exalted

falling for, falling in, falling out of love
reality shimmering in the dim light
even as battles for self
carried unimaginable prices

We paid our admission
in the coin of silence
living in the sty of prejudice
and still...
we danced like gladiators
upon the spines of our fear
feet sliding smooth in the
slippery guts of the monster
beneath our beds
we danced the night away
shimmy shimmy shimmy
shake your groove thang
yeah yeah yeah

It was there
inside the skeleton
of another ancestor
that the dancing Queens
the Trans, the Fairies, the Dykes
all the children, pushed back
until the right to say "I do"

became the law of the land
a right perched precariously among the
sharpened stakes of bigotry
aimed at tender throats
married on Sunday
fired on Monday

Reminded yet again
that it's never over
amid the waning hours
of a hot summer night
a festering, rotted heart
fanning the forges of
hatred's flaming lust
giving birth to metal winged
birds of prey / harbingers of death
splitting the world wide open
tearing apart the fragile fantasy
of somehow / someway / belonging

Spewing destruction
45 bullets per minute
minute, after minute, after minute
until when it was done
49 lay without a pulse
53 more stutter stepping

between worlds
pulses flickering as the bullets
tore through their innocence
and even then it was not enough
of a blood sacrifice for those pulpits
preaching hatred in the guise of love

Blood. Soaked. Horror.
screams
terror
grief
funerals
tears
candlelight shrines
forever empty chairs
in 49 homes
all the talking heads chattering
incessantly
and still nothing changed
for guns or rights
equality but a dream of the 49
equality but a dream
of those they left behind
and you can still buy that gun
All / Day / Long
while dreaming about

what seems to be
the impossible dream

When you wish upon a star
maybe one day
it really won't matter
who you are

BUTCH WITH A CAPITAL B

She fastens the top button
of her dress shirt then wraps designer silk
around her collar where it is
pulled up snug into a Windsor knot

Over her boxers she slides on
a pair of trousers
that sport perfect creases with one-inch cuffs
that hit her shoe tops just so

Like a gunslinger she wraps
her dark leather belt
around her waist, buckle gleaming bright

She checks her shoes to gauge
their shine then buffs
an errant toe on the back of her calf

She stands looking in the mirror, legs astride
carefully combing her hair, checking its trim

Shrugging into her suit coat
she shoots her cuffs
making sure her cufflinks are showing

She straightens her tie one last time
then opens the door
stepping outside into the
blast furnace of a world that tries to
melt down her butchness
she is her own queer politic
the in-your-face
I will not hide
this is who I am

STEP-SISTER'S LAMENT

I didn't even want
to go to the ball
wearing this
ridiculous dress
that mother and sister
think is so posh

Their dreams of
snagging a prince
not one of my own

I wanted to wear
long pants with
shiny black boots
a pirate shirt
billowing cape
with a saber
rattling at my side

Sans face paint
and curled wig
wearing only a
roguish smile
upon my lips as

I asked her to dance
this beauty I knew
as Cinderella
into whose
home I'd been thrust
by mother's marriage
to her father

The first time that I saw her
amid introductions all round
in morning's light
among the roses of her garden
my heart lurched so
that I thought
myself about to die

From that moment on
I lived for the sound
of her voice and
every waking moment
I sought reason
to spend with her
until her father's
untimely death

And yes...

I do wonder about that
when her life forever
changed in this house
from sibling to servant
under mother's cruelty
that is such I dare not
attempt to play the hero

So here I sit alone
in this cage of the
feminine silk and tulle
watching her waltz
across the room with
the kingdom's prince
knowing in this moment
that I will never be
a suitor for her heart

Mother arrives
admonishments fly
sit up straight
straighten your gown
smile pretty or
at least pretend
you're having a good time for
the gentlemen here

It's likely you'll never
gain a prince
but a husband
of some kind
must be had

I watch her twirl
around the room
so light and beautiful
in his arms
that I desperately
long to be mine

Her rescue is at hand
while there is none
to be had for me...

But, but... hold up!
Wait a minute!
Who's the Princess
that just came in?

I bet mother would
be just as happy
with a Princess
even if she is a girl

Eyes meet, heart leaps
Once upon a time
in a land far away

WHEN I WAS THIRTEEN

The screaming
that's the worst part
that and the Thorazine Shuffle
stagger stagger
drool drool
nodding like
you got them
junkie blues
but it's always
full circle back
to the screaming
their royal majesties
holding high court
as the madness roils
through tender brains
until the only
voice that is left
is to scream
some just stand
and scream
some run and scream
some swing fists
and scream
some do all three

every single day.

I am terrified.

Every. Single. Day.

PHILLY

I heard the name of a city
Philadelphia
repeated three times in one hour
the third from a poet
who got everything and everyone he loves
from poetry
especially
his husband

My brain synapsed into long forgotten connections
how could I have forgotten
I swore that I never would
as a string quartet
began to play on the radio
and it made me think
of you and the many others
returned to the ashes
from whence you came
long before it was your time
to set your ship's bow
toward the horizon
homeward bound
if there is such a thing

I thought of that movie *Philadelphia*
where Andrew fights back
against those who shamed his illness
your illness
the first time that we could see on the big screen
all of the suffering
the bigotry, the hatred
that you knew
firsthand

I went home and I played the aria from the movie
"La Mamma Morta"
the house was burning down
all around us
in those long-ago days
when you joked about being my gay husband
and we held our breaths in hopefulness
mixed with T-cells and
pharmaceutical cocktails

I cried again
tears as hot and full as the tail of a comet
burning the sorrow
into bone where though long unseen
is branded with your name
with all of your brethren, dearly beloved

etched into femur, ulna, shin and skull
forever, indelibly, upon my heart
since the day you left

LONOKE

Sun lit up for gloryland
sky smooth baby blue
belying the solemnness
of those gathering
standing
hip-and-shoulder deep
in a small country chapel
where for just a moment
all hearts beat together
a rhythm of shared sorrow
grief that transcended
politics and Jesus
as family, queers,
and church folk alike
listened to Dolly Parton
while a true Lonoke
Southern girl lay in state
bejeweled in glitter glam
eyeliner wings on point
receiving tear-stained tributes
as mourners one by one
bid their loving adieus
an old dyke slips a pin
that says BUTCH into her hand

a last good-bye
to a fierce femme friend

From the pulpit comes
measured tones
of pastoral reassurance
hawking heaven's delights
then an aunt with a message
from her MeMe
one of boundless love
gutted loss and sweet tea
a *bless your heart*
to the bigots and the haters
while those who've been targets
whisper "right on!" and do little
fist pumps behind the pews

Kleenex, a commodity of
kinship and kindness
as church ladies pass
tissues to weeping queens
and the lines of difference
fleetingly disappear
until that final song
that final prayer
and then amen

and all rise
exiting into the light
that will never be
quite the same again
that honeyed, Southern *y'all*
forever gone, radio silent

Amanda Beth Harris
October 3, 1984 – September 23, 2016

IN TIME

This watch
tells time
decorates
my wrist
weighty
in its gold
and silver
presence
but it's neither
jewelry nor
timekeeper

it's forgiveness

the first taste
of understanding

it's an exhale
a moment
when I knew
that my mother
truly saw me

when shopping
one day she

took me—her
only daughter
to the counter
where men
shop for watches
and helped me
pick out
this watch
that tells
time very well
both hands
pointing right
at the moment
that I knew
my mother saw me
and loved me
completely

THE KIND OF WOMAN I AM

The kind of woman I am
dreams of fiery red tulips
pushing through snow-covered ground
like bloody fingers reaching up
for the sun to pull down close to earth
melting the frozen tundra
that locks away the roots of justice
from all the people who have been strange fruit
whipped
pushed
shoved
driven
marched
and turned out from the table
set in gold plate and fine linen.

The kind of woman I am
dreams of a place
where there's enough for all
and children don't wail in the night with rats
biting at their toes
bloody fingers grabbing at the feet
of soldiers and warmongers.

The kind of woman I am
dreams of grinding their tanks into dust.

I dream of these bloody fingers that say
Think not that I am come
to send peace on earth.
I came not to send peace,
but a sword.

I dream of blazing red fingers
that strip away the masks of the greedy
that are setting those with little against those without.

Such dreams as these toss me around my bed
sheets all a-tangle
sweating with the struggle
till I'm thrown to the floor
where I pull on my boots
and go outside
to plant tulips.

ABOUT THE POET

Randi M. Romo has a voice that reaches into multiple segments of who we are as humans, with an emphasis on queer. As a working-class Mexican-American, Southerner, former farmworker, organizer/activist, female, parent, grandparent, elder, and survivor, she has walked among and between many communities.

Romo truly believes that it is only by hearing one another and sharing with one another that we have any hope to traverse the vast chasms of differences, real and perceived, that extend beyond our immediate realities. She likes to say that the power of love requires tending, like any garden. It is a bloom that must be watered with knowledge, fed truth under the sun of trust, and harvested in justice. She hopes that her words are a part of the seedlings working their way toward the understandings that sprout mighty oaks of love.

ABOUT THE PRESS

Sibling Rivalry Press is an independent press based in Little Rock, Arkansas. It is a sponsored project of Fractured Atlas, a nonprofit arts service organization. Contributions to support the operations of Sibling Rivalry Press are tax-deductible to the extent permitted by law. To contribute to the publication of more books like this one, please visit our website and click *donate*.

We gratefully acknowledge the following donors, without whom this book would not be possible:

Liz Ahl

Stephanie Anderson

Priscilla Atkins

John Bateman

Sally Bellerose & Cynthia Suopis

Jen Benka

Dustin Brookshire

Sarah Browning

Russell Bunge

Michelle Castleberry

Don Cellini

Philip F. Clark

Risa Denenberg

Alex Gildzen

J. Andrew Goodman

Sara Gregory

Karen Hayes

Wayne B. Johnson & Marcos L. Martínez

Jessica Manack

Alicia Mountain

Rob Jacques

Nahal Suzanne Jamir

Bill La Civita

Mollie Lacy

Anthony Lioi

Catherine Lundoff

Adrian M.

Ed Madden

Open Mouth Reading Series

Red Hen Press

Steven Reigns

Paul Romero

Erik Schuckers

Alana Smoot

Stillhouse Press

KMA Sullivan

Billie Swift

Tony Taylor

Hugh Tipping

Eric Tran

Ursus Americanus Press

Julie Marie Wade

Ray Warman & Dan Kiser

Anonymous (14)

CPSIA information can be obtained
at www.ICGtesting.com
Printed in the USA
FFOW02n0803210718
47469992-50723FF